Why Do I Hiccup?

by Molly Kolpin

Consulting Editor: Gail Saunders-Smith, PhD

Consultant: Marjorie Hogan, MD
Department of Pediatrics
Hennepin County Medical Center

CAPSTONE PRESS
a capstone imprint

Pebble® Plus

Pebble Plus is published by Capstone Press,
1710 Roe Crest Drive, North Mankato, Minnesota 56003
www.capstonepub.com

Library of Congress Cataloging-in-Publication Data
Kolpin, Molly, author.
Why do I hiccup? / by Molly Kolpin.
pages cm. — (Pebble plus. My silly body)
Summary: "Simple text and colorful images describe what happens in the body when we hiccup and how to get rid of them"— Provided by publisher.
Audience: Ages 4–8.
Audience: K to grade 3.
Includes bibliographical references and index.
ISBN 978-1-4914-2106-2 (library binding)
ISBN 978-1-4914-2347-9 (eBook PDF)
1. Hiccups—Juvenile literature. 2. Reflexes—Juvenile literature. I. Title.
QP372.K565 2015
612.8'9—dc23   2014022199

Editorial Credits
Michelle Hasselius, editor; Kazuko Collins, designer; Gina Kammer, media researcher; Morgan Walters, production specialist

Photo Credits
Alamy: Bubbles Photolibrary, 19; Capstone Studio: Karon Dubke, cover; Dreamstime: Kenishirotie, 11, Murali Nath, 13, Pipa100, 17; Shutterstock: AJP, 9, ffoto29, 21, Sebastian Kaulitzki, 7, szefei, 5, Tyler Olson, 15
Design Elements: Shutterstock: Eliks (spotted design), Milanares (sun flare)

Note to Parents and Teachers

The My Silly Body set supports national science standards related to life science. This book describes and illustrates why we hiccup. The images support early readers in understanding the text. The repetition of words and phrases helps early readers learn new words. This book also introduces early readers to subject-specific vocabulary words, which are defined in the Glossary section. Early readers may need assistance to read some words and to use the Table of Contents, Glossary, Read More, Internet Sites, and Index sections of the book.

Printed in the United States of America in Stevens Point, Wisconsin.
102014   008479WZS15

Table of Contents

Hic-Hic-Hiccup!

Why do I hiccup?
You hiccup when your
diaphragm tightens suddenly.
Everyone from babies to
adults gets the hiccups!

Scientists think babies can hiccup before they are born.

Your diaphragm is a muscle
under your lungs. It helps
you breathe by pushing air
in and out of your body.

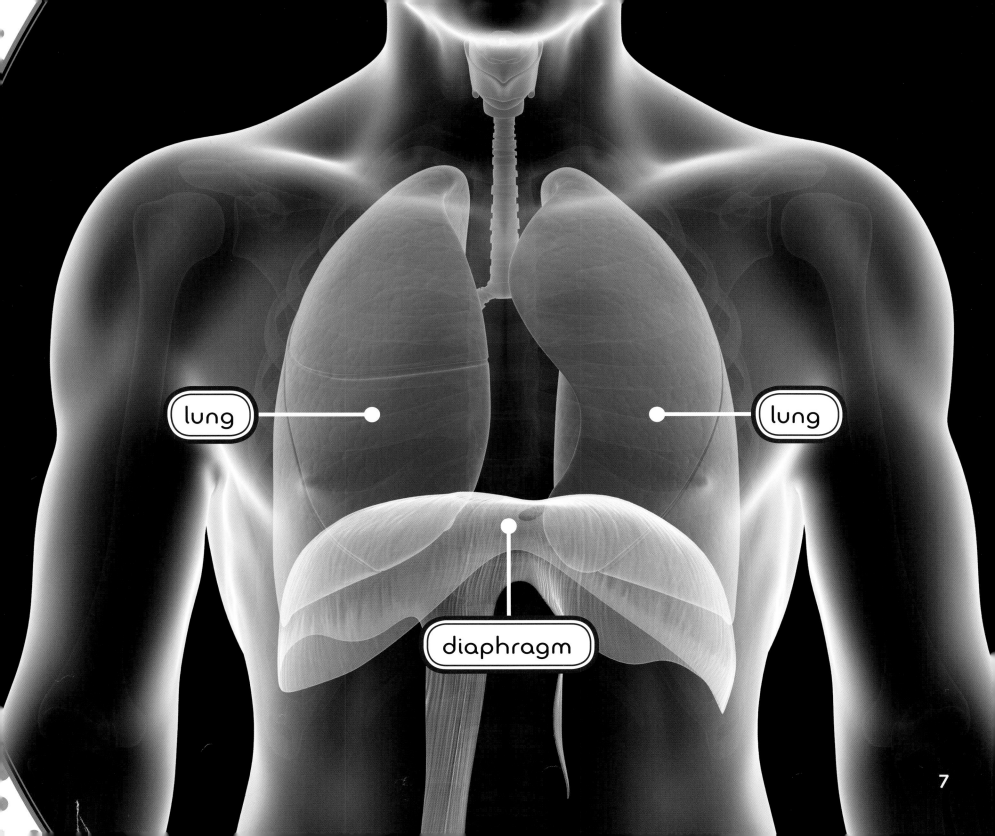

lung

lung

diaphragm

When your diaphragm gets tight, you breathe in extra air. The air hits the voice box in your throat. This can cause the hiccup sound.

You can't see your voice box when you open your mouth. But it helps you speak and make sounds.

9

The Diaphragm Diaries

You can get hiccups after eating or drinking too much. Your stomach swells and pushes against your diaphragm. This pressure tightens your diaphragm and you hiccup.

You can also get hiccups by eating too quickly. Take small bites and chew food slowly.

Hiccups can happen when you are surprised or feel nervous. Your nerves react to these feelings and can cause your diaphragm to tighten.

Healing Your Hiccups

Hiccups usually go away
after a few minutes. But most
people don't want to wait.
They try to cure their hiccups.

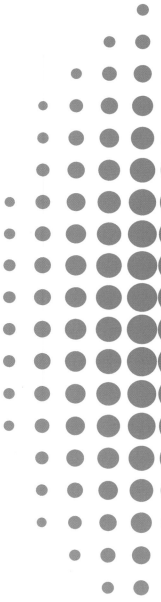

Some people believe a spoonful of sugar can cure hiccups.

One cure is to hold your
breath for 10 seconds. This
tells your body you need
more air. Your body stops
hiccuping to focus on breathing.

A possible hiccup cure is to plug your ears and drink a glass of water.

Another cure is to drink
water from the other side of
the glass. This can get messy,
but it might stop your hiccups.

Boo!

Surprises may cause and cure hiccups. Ask someone to scare away your hiccups by yelling, "Boo!" This famous cure may really work!

Remember not everyone likes to be scared when they have hiccups.

21

Glossary

cure—a way to make someone feel better

diaphragm—the muscle under your lungs that moves as you breathe

lung—an organ inside the chest used to breathe

muscle—a part of your body that helps you move, lift, or push

nerve—a fiber that takes messages from your brain to other parts of your body

pressure—the force made by pressing on something

surprise—the feeling caused by something unexpected

voice box—the part of your throat that contains your vocal cords

Read More

Allyn, Daisy. *What Happens When I Hiccup?* My Body Does Strange Stuff! New York: Gareth Stevens Publishing, 2014.

Fromer, Liza, and Francine Gerstein. *My Noisy Body.* Body Works. Toronto: Tundra Books, 2011.

Royston, Angela. *Twitches and Sneezes.* Disgusting Body Facts. Chicago: Raintree, 2010.

Internet Sites

FactHound offers a safe, fun way to find Internet sites related to this book. All of the sites on FactHound have been researched by our staff.

Here's all you do:

Visit *www.facthound.com*

Type in this code: 9781491421062

Super-cool stuff! Check out projects, games and lots more at www.capstonekids.com

Your diaphragm is a muscle in your body that helps you breathe. How does your diaphragm cause hiccups? (Key Ideas and Details)

Many people get hiccups. Think back to a time when you had hiccups. How did you get rid of them? (Integration of Knowledge and Ideas)

Index

Word Count: 206
Grade: 1
Early-Intervention Level: 20